T0198685

God's Majesty In Nature

JOHN TRAVASSOS

WestBow Press books may be ordered through booksellers or by contacting:

WestBow Press
A Division of Thomas Nelson & Zondervan
1663 Liberty Drive
Bloomington, IN 47403
www.westbowpress.com
844-714-3454

ISBN: 978-1-6642-7157-9 (sc)
ISBN: 978-1-6642-7158-6 (e)

Library of Congress Control Number: 2022912338

Print information available on the last page.

WestBow Press rev. date: 9/23/2022

WESTBOW
PRESS®
A DIVISION OF THOMAS NELSON
& ZONDERVAN

I dedicate this book to my grandchildren and to my wife, Michelle, without whose encouragement this book would never have been created.

And, of course, to God who has opened my eyes to the majesty of His creation.

In the beginning, God created the heavens and the earth.

-Genesis 1:1 (ESV)

Praise the Lord!
Praise the Lord from the heavens
praise him in the heights!
Praise him, all his angels;
praise him, all his hosts!

Praise him, sun and moon,
praise him, all you shining stars!
Praise him, you highest heavens,
and you waters above the heavens!

Let them praise the name of the Lord!
For he commanded and they were created
And he established them forever and ever;
he gave a decree, and it shall not pass away.

Praise the Lord from the earth,
you great sea creatures and all deeps,
fire and hail, snow and mist,
stormy wind fulfilling his word!

Mountains and all hills,
fruit trees and all cedars!
Beasts and all livestock,
creeping things and flying birds!

Kings of the earth and all peoples,
princes and all rulers of the earth!
Young men and maidens together,
old men and children!

Let them praise the name of the Lord,
for his name alone is exalted.
his majesty is above earth and heaven.

He has raised up a horn for his people,
praise for all his saints
for the people of Israel who are near to him.
Praise the Lord!

-Psalm 148 (ESV)

Within each acorn lives a forest.

The Majesty of God in Nature

Dear Reader,

Since I was ten years old, I have been a constant observer of nature, and I am a believer in God our Creator. I decided to write this book for all the boys and girls like you to introduce you to the possibility that you will see God in nature like I and others do. As identified in the opening scripture, all the things that God has made show His majesty, from the stars in the skies to the fish in the ocean, through beautiful landscapes to fascinating creatures, plants, and animals. By observing these fascinating natural things, we can understand that God is real and that He is supreme. You can find examples of God's creation right in your backyard.

Throughout this book I will provide Bible scriptures along with examples from nature to illustrate this point. I hope that you will discover how the amazing things in nature reflect the creative power and love of God. God wants us to meditate on-think deeply about-what we discover.

Once God created the earth and all its creatures, He saw it as good. He instructed us to take care of it, to use it wisely, and not to abuse it or use it for our greed. As such, we have a responsibility as guardians to treat the earth as a gardener would treat his or her garden-with care, so that nothing is wasted and used for evil purposes. After all, we humans are the ones who benefit from His Creation. Scripture is clear in how God cares perfectly for His creation, including the wild beasts and the flowers, so we should have confidence in God caring for us, since we are made in God's image.

My hope is that you will enjoy the discoveries in this book and those you will open your eyes to in the coming months and years. As you study God and nature, look for the wisdom He provides through nature in scripture. The entire natural world bears witness to God through its beauty, complexity, design, and usefulness.

I have enjoyed writing it for you.

Blessings,
John Travassos

The Loop, the Microscope, and Binoculars

Throughout my life I have had the opportunity to view God's creation through helpful instruments. I've owned all three of these fun instruments, and I've been awed by what I have seen through them. I hope you will have the opportunity to use one or all of these instruments to get closer to nature, because the closer you look into nature, the more you will see God's handiwork.

Whether you're looking into the secrets of cells with a microscope or out searching for birds in nearby fields with your binoculars, each instrument will help reveal the secrets of God's creations. Of all these instruments, I have found the magnifying loop (also known as a jeweler's loop) to be the most useful. It's easy to use and can be carried in your pocket, ready to be used at any moment.

To use the loop, hold it up to your eye, and bring the object you want to examine closer until it comes in focus. That's it! I typically use a lanyard to carry my loop so it's handy to get to. Carry it with you whenever you're out and about on hikes, visits to the seashore, or anywhere else you go to enjoy nature. It will open up a new world that you might not normally see.

In his hand are the depths of the earth; the heights of the mountains are his also. The sea is his, for he made it, and his hands formed the dry land.

-Psalm 95:4-5 (ESV)

Of the trillions of trillions (1,000,000,000,000,000,000 ,000,000) of celestial bodies in the universe, God created one special place for all living things- the Earth, which is part of our solar system and traveling through space at 448,000 miles per hour. It's the only place in the universe where God placed all the elements required to support life. And in this one special place, God chose to create and place humanity in His image. Again, think about that for a moment. Out of trillions of places, God chose Earth as our home. Therefore, we should honor His creation of Earth and realize just how special of a place it is.

Scientists estimate that there may be between 8 and 10 million living species on and in the land and waters of the Earth, of which only 1.3 million have been identified. Experts estimate that it could take more than one thousand years to identify all of them. Below are some of the estimates of different species. How many do you know or will you discover?

375,000 species of plants (on average 2,500 new species are identified each year)

80,000 species of algae

1,000 species of barnacles

10,000 species of ants

18,000 species of birds (on average only 10 new species are identified each year)

34,000 species of fish (on average 250 new species are identified each year)

The list is virtually endless, so there's no shortage of opportunity for you to explore and discover God's majesty in His creation.

I would recommend you watch Louie Giglio's YouTube video "If the Earth Were the Size of a Golf Ball".

It's fun and fascinating. For example, Louie suggests that if the Earth were the size of a golf ball, it would take 960,000 golf balls to fill the sun. This is equivalent to filling a school bus with golf balls. Giglio's video will help you further understand the size of God's universe and how special the Earth is.

In order to care for the Earth, we have to understand how the natural systems of the Earth function. The health of both humanity and the Earth are dependent on understanding and caring for it. So it's important to learn as much as you can about the Earth and its inhabitants and places. Let's now continue to learn more about God's creation here on Earth.

So God created great sea creatures and every living thing that scurries and swarms in the water, and every sort of bird—each producing offspring of the same kind. And God saw that it was good.

-Genesis 1:21 (NLT)

It's low tide, seagulls are pecking along the exposed shoreline for food, and a dense fog is rolling in. There are rocks and sand, wet from the light rain; small waves reach the edge of land, and everything casts a gray hue. These are days that I love to be at the shore. Most of us encounter the shoreline when we visit the sunny beach, but for me these damp, dreary days offer solace from an otherwise busy place. It's just me and God's creatures. But for the occasional raucous call of a gull and the rhythmic sounds of the waves, quiet is what I find.

And I ask myself, "Why did God create the seagulls?" Actually, I wonder why God created any of the many creatures that live here, including those in the vast ocean. I imagine it full of creatures, from microscopic plankton to the world's largest creature, the blue whale. Scientists estimate there are a million sea creatures. And besides being home to all these creatures, the ocean provides more than 50 percent of the Earth's oxygen, part of the air we need to breathe and fill our lungs. Then I remember Psalm 148, which says that all His creatures sing His praises. And Psalm 98 declares, "Let the sea roar, and all that fills it." Why not? Doesn't God deserve the glory for all His creation?

Nothing is by accident in nature. If He has chosen to take care of all these creatures, what do you imagine He has done for us? Like the creatures, we should sing the praises of the Lord.

I strongly suggest that you and your family watch the amazing video by Lou Giglio called "Stars and Whales Singing How Great Is Our God."

But ask the beasts, and they will teach you; the birds of the heavens, and they will tell you; or the bushes of the earth, and they will teach you; and the fish of the sea will declare to you. Who among all these does not know that the hand of the Lord has done this? In his hand is the life of every living thing and the breath of all mankind.

-Job 12:7-10 (ESV)

The Bees

I think most of us are fascinated by bees. Bees have an interesting life story. One bee only lives between one and two months, and in that time it visits hundreds if not thousands of flowers collecting nectar and pollen, making about a teaspoon of honey for all its effort. As the bee seeks food (nectar) from the flowers, tiny pollen particles attach to the bee's legs, hitching a ride to the next flower of the same kind. Pollen from the previous flower is now spread to the next flower, fertilizing it, thereby spreading life. Twenty thousand different kinds of bees ensure that plants across the world continue to thrive. Much of the food we eat relies on bees pollinating it to bring forth fruits and vegetables. The bees provide a free service that God uses to sustain our life and those of other creatures, as we find nourishment from the food bees help create. And who doesn't like honey anyway?

In this short time, the bee has fulfilled its destiny, just as God intended.

God has planted in you a destiny as well.

So what might your destiny be?

Swarms of living creatures will live wherever the river flows. There will be large numbers of fish, because this water flows there and makes the salt water fresh; so where the river flows everything will live.

-Ezekiel 47:9 (NIV)

Maybe you've seen TV programs in which fish are swimming and jumping upstream in turbulent waters. This is an annual event on many streams and rivers. Some of these fish return from the ocean where they've been living for several years, growing to adulthood, and now they're returning to their exact home streams for spawning, giving birth to the next generation of fish.

I am amazed to think how it can be possible for the fish to find their home, especially after traveling for thousands of miles in the open ocean. They don't have built-in GPS maps, do they? How is it, then, that God created such creatures with such amazing capabilities? Scientists can only speculate as to how these fish accomplish such an intricate task. Do they read the stars? Do they taste certain chemicals in the water? How do you think the fish find their way home? God is precise in His designs.

On the glorious splendor of your majesty, and on your wonderous works, I will meditate.

-Psalm 145:5 (ESV)

There's a slight chill in the air of this early September morning along the coast of Maine, and my wife and I are enjoying the flower gardens of the place we are staying at while on vacation. Dozens of colorful flowers decorate the garden area, and among them on a bright red flower we spot our first Monarch. Monarchs are always a beautiful site to bear. In its short lifetime, the butterfly will visit and pollinate thousands of flowers. But autumn is coming quickly, so I wonder why this Monarch hasn't

already started its journey south for the winter. Or maybe it has. As always, I wonder how it is that this little insect, without a brain, knows when it's time to head to its winter home in Mexico. Though scientists have several theories about this, the question remains unsolved, so the mystery remains.

A Monarch born in northern North America, will travel more than a thousand miles to a small plot of land located in the high mountains of Mexico where they spend the winter with millions of other Monarchs before returning northward the following springtime. Those that head northward will never make it back to the wintering grounds in Mexico. On their northward journey, however, the Monarch breeds, lay eggs only on the backside of milkweed leaves, and then dies, leaving the new butterflies that are hatched to move onward. It is these new offspring that will continue to fly northward. But since Monarchs live only between six and nine months, even those will not likely be the ones to make it back to Mexico. So, how does a Monarch who has never been to Mexico find its way there?

As we have no conclusive explanation for how the Monarch completes this extraordinary journey, we can trust in God's plan. All creatures were created by God with a purpose to bring glory to our Father in heaven. The Monarch's fascinating journey certainly displays God's majesty and glorifies Him.

Keep an eye out for the Monarch in your neighborhood, and then consider what great purpose and plan God might have in store for you? You too are a marvelous creation.

Consider the lilies, how they grow: they neither toil nor spin, yet I tell you, even Solomon in all his glory was not arrayed like one of these.

-Luke 12:27 (ESV)

Is there anything more joyful than a beautiful flower? We take pictures of them, we give them to celebrate special occasions, we smell them, and we pick them for our moms. Flowers have inspired writers, artists, and poets. And Jesus tells us to learn from them. So why *did* God dress the land with them? Yes, they serve a biological function, especially when it comes to attracting insects and birds for pollination purposes. But doesn't it seem that God may have also created them to bring beauty to the world and to display His majesty?

The earth brought forth vegetation, plants yielding seed according to their own kinds, and trees bearing fruit in which is their seed, each according to its kind. And God saw that it was good.

-Genesis 1:12 (ESV)

Do you see God's majesty in the leaf?

God created the leaf, a wonderous way in which He supports life in the world. The leaf produces food for the trees and shrubs by converting sunlight into sugar. And in the leaf's processing of food, it generates a significant source of oxygen, which most living things need to survive, including me, you, and all animals. Scientists estimate that there are approximately 375,000 different plants, most of which have leaves.

As the sunlight fades in the autumn, the leaves of many trees lose their ability to maintain their green color. Then the leaves show the underlying colors, the reds, oranges, and yellows we see in the fall. This provides us with the annual beauty that artists and photographers try to capture every year when we all go out on our leaf-peeping trips.

As with the flowers, this display of color is based on biology, but God saw to it that we would find beauty in this time of the year by painting the landscape for our enjoyment. Where else do you see God's majesty on display?

For every beast of the forest is mine, and the cattle on a thousand hills. I know all the birds of the hills, and all that moves in the field is mine.

-Psalm 50:10-11 (ESV)

Today I watched a beautiful bird visit a bush full of clusters of red berries. I have studied this, and did you know that there's kind of a secret relationship between the birds and such bushes? While the bird finds nourishment from the berries, the seeds in the bird's stomach catch a free ride to wherever the bird alights next and poops, planting the seeds for a new crop of bushes in that location. What an ingenious way to spread the seeds! Birds are not the only animals that provide for the dispersal of seeds, but they are one of the most obvious.

Grab your binoculars and head to the forests and fields, especially in the winter months, looking for birds feeding on berries. If you find them, you are witnessing cleverness at work. Yes, this majestic relationship meets the needs of the birds and that of the shrubs at the same time. God is a master at relationships.

The insects in the fields are mine.

-Psalm 50:11 (NIV)

On late summer days, I often hear cicadas singing their loud buzzing sounds from the treetops. These are unusual insects, with some of them (brood X) living underground for seventeen years before emerging and singing their songs. It's only the male cicada that sings. He calls out trying to impress a potential girlfriend. He's also claiming his territory to other males. Have you heard them? As a child, I always took the arrival of their sound as a signal that we were past the height of summer, with autumn not too far away. But I wonder how the cicadas know when seventeen years are up.

Do they have a clock or calendar? Of course not. The majesty of God can be seen in this seemingly inexplicable event of nature. Maybe someday scientists will figure out how this all works; for now they can only speculate on why this happens. But meanwhile we can be astonished by nature's unique displays and trust in God's perfect timing.

For his invisible attributes, namely, his eternal power and divine nature, have been clearly perceived, ever since the creation of the world, in the things that have been made. So they are without excuse.

-Romans 1:20 (ESV)

The Fibonacci Sequence

I don't know about you, but while I excelled at science, I was not very good at math. For some reason, I always had a hard time connecting math to my life. Then I learned about the Fibonacci sequence, which is widely represented in nature. I realized that God used mathematics in His creation! The sequence is a series of numbers that are related to one another—0, 1, 1, 2, 3, 5, 8, 13, 21, 34, 55, 89, 144, and so forth. Look carefully; each number in the sequence is the sum of the previous two numbers. When these numbers appear in a geometric (think shapes) pattern, they exhibit fascinating features found in animals, plants, and even the stars.

As the following photos reveal, the shell of the nautilus shows a spiral design. The galaxy's spiral, the ram's horn, and the sunflower seed patterns all follow the sequence. These are just a few of the things in nature that represent the Fibonacci sequence. You can find several books on the Fibonacci sequence in nature.

The next time you go out into nature, keep an eye out for this pattern

There are many other mathematical patterns in nature as well. You can study more about these as you grow in knowledge about God in nature. I guess God likes math as well as nature. He uses math to form and display His majesty. And now I see math entirely differently, and I am astonished how intricate and detailed God's designs are.

O Lord, what a variety of things you have made! In wisdom you have made them all. The earth is full of your creatures.

-Psalm 104:24 (NLT)

The Ant and the Universe of God

Today I studied a small ant nest, looking at one of the ten thousand species of ants in the world. It was a little mound of dirt shaped in a cone with a small hole at its center, and it reminded me of the shape of a tiny volcano. I saw ants scurrying in and out of the hole at the same time. Ants play an important role in the ecosystem. They till the ground, they help decompose organic matter, and they recycle nutrients through the ground. They help rainwater penetrate the ground. Without ants, the world would be different. Many plants and animals would be affected.

As people, we go about our daily lives and rarely, if ever, ponder our place in the universe and how God saw fit to place us here on this one little planet. Here, in His image, we live out our busy lives going here and there, hardly thinking about how or why we are here. It's easy to be distracted by all the busyness of living.

And yet there is this tiny ant nest by my feet, also holding a special place in this universe that God created.

Where's your place in the world? What role do you play in God's creation? What's your purpose?

For, "Who has known the mind of the Lord so as to instruct him?" But we have the mind of Christ.

-1 Corinthians 2:16 (NIV)

Sometimes what seems obvious is not so. The Bible says we can know the mind of God if we have the spirit of Christ in us, which gives us discernment. Look at these two images of cattails; both occupy wet areas and are used as food and home by many wildlife species. Do they look alike? Yes. Are they the same? No. They are two different species of plants that grow in different habitats. A close study of them would reveal that they have differences in structure and shape. The broad-leafed cattails (top) typically grow in freshwater marshes, while the narrow-leaved cattail grows in environments that are more brackish (salty). Yet they look

virtually the same! God makes no mistakes. He intentionally designed these two plants to occupy different types of habitats. We are all members of the human race, but each of us is different as well, and each of us has his or her own destiny to fulfill. What will your destiny be?

Afterword

These examples of God's creations should be the start of your journey to find examples of the majesty of God in nature. So grab your loop, binoculars, or microscope and dive into searching and discovering. Maybe someday you will be a scientist searching the Earth, or you could be an amateur naturalist searching out the millions of plants and animals inhabiting the Earth. Whichever path you decide to take, trust that God will direct you.

As you move on from this book, I encourage you to continue your study of nature and the Bible. You should read your Bible every day, and when the opportunity comes, you should study nature. There are countless excellent books about nature. There are many field guides about flowers and plants, birds, wildlife, seashells, butterflies, and so forth that will take you virtually anywhere in the world and show you much about the plants and animals that live in the area. As you now know, there are millions of plants and animals and rocks and natural things waiting to be discovered.

Knowing about nature makes a visit to the beach more than just an opportunity for swimming. Searching the tidal pools for all sorts of creatures, including crabs, clams, seaweeds, and so forth, makes for an enjoyable adventure. Going for a hike in the forest becomes a journey of discovery. Remember to bring along your loop or your binoculars.

I hope this book has inspired you to see God through nature and that you will be more aware of how God created all things through His power and for His majesty and glory.

God bless you on your journeys.

April 2022

PS: I have included a few examples of my favorite creations of God.

And out of the ground the LORD God made to spring up every tree that is pleasant to the sight and good for food.

-Genesis 2:9(ESV)

My favorite tree is the tamarack. It is typically found in cooler northern climates here in the United States. It is a fascinating tree to me for several reasons. First, I love the smoky gold color it turns in the autumn. It stands among other pine trees that usually remain green in the autumn and winter, so the tamarack really sticks out when it turns gold. I am also fond of the fact that is only one of a few pine trees that actually loses its leaves in the autumn. Most pine trees retain their leaves all winter long, but not the tamarack. Lastly, when you see a cluster of tamarack leaves up close, you will notice that the cluster is not typical of most pine trees. They are unique.

The tamarack offers a celebration of color in the otherwise green pine forests and reminds me of how God clothes His land in many colors, bringing us pleasure in viewing and enjoying them in their natural state.

*Let the heavens rejoice, let the earth be glad;
let the sea resound, and all that is in it.
Let the fields be jubilant, and everything
in them; let all the trees of the forest sing
for joy.*

-Psalm 96:11-12 (NIV)

The black-capped chickadee is my favorite bird. I encounter it often when walking in the woods, and it even shows up at the bird feeder at my apartment in the city.

When I was a young boy, my father told me that this was a Johnny bird because to him, the bird's call, "fee-bee," sounded like Johnny. So since that time, I have called it a Johnny bird. My wife says differently. She says it's a Jesus bird. Either way it is my favorite little bird.

Do you have a favorite bird, favorite tree, or favorite animal? Maybe it's something entirely different. The point is that God created these beautiful creatures for our enjoyment. I hope you have some favorites of your own.

The wilderness and the dry land shall be glad; the desert shall rejoice and blossom like the crocus; it shall blossom abundantly and rejoice with joy and singing.

-Isaiah 35:1-2 (ESV)

As we have seen before in this book, flowers are special. They decorate the landscape. The desert gold poppy is one of my favorite flowers. When the spring flowers bloom in the desert, especially after a good wet winter, the display is breathtaking. Acres and acres of these flowers cover the landscape, bringing great beauty to the otherwise drab land. It is a time of great celebration when this happens. I look forward to my visits to the desert in the springtime.

Meeting at Lloyd's Beach, Little Compton, Rhode Island

I heard the waves claim Your presence in
Praise after praise.
Glittering ocean showed Your light in
Praise after praise.
Deep-blue sky carried a song across the heavens in
Praise after praise.
Despite a chilled north wind, your sun offered warmth in
Praise after praise.
I told you how I see You in
Praise after praise.
I thanked You for the gift in
Praise after praise.
You received my hope, and I gave in
Praise after praise.
Long we chatted, and You gave more in
Praise after praise.

I heard Your voice amid the chorus in
Praise after praise.
No greater symphony can be heard in
Praise after praise.
Thank You for Your majesty in
Praise after praise.
I raised my eyes and hands in
Praise after praise.
I bowed my head, thankful, in
Praise after praise.
And as I departed, the shrill of a seaside sparrow sang in
Praise after praise.
All showed Your glory in
Praise after praise.
Praise be to You, Lord.

-John Travassos, March 9, 2021

Printed in the United States
by Baker & Taylor Publisher Services